Damon Burnard

*Hodder
Children's
Books*

a division of Hodder Headline plc

Johnny, Larissa
and Sabrina

Copyright © 1996 Damon Burnard

First published in Great Britain in 1996
by Hodder Children's Books

10 9 8 7 6 5 4

A Catalogue record for this book is available from the British Library

ISBN 0-340-64855-4

Typeset by Avon Dataset Ltd, Bidford-on-Avon B50 4JH

Printed and bound in Great Britain by
Cox & Wyman Ltd, Reading, Berks.

Hodder Children's Books
A division of Hodder Headline plc
338 Euston Road
London NW1 3BH

CHAPTER ONE

One day, in the year 1896, world-famous dinosaur expert, Professor Henry Water-Biscuit, was searching for fossils in the desert. His assistant, Carlisle Withering, was helping.

In the middle of the afternoon, the professor's shovel struck something hard. "Oh my goodness!" he gasped.

The professor pointed a trembling finger.

Breathlessly, they swept it clean.

Carlisle and the professor heaved open the stone cover. "Before you look at my recipes," it said in giant, looping handwriting, "I ask that you read this . . ."

They fell to their knees in the scarlet soil and, eyes wide with wonder, began to read. And this is what it said . . .

CHAPTER TWO

Once upon a time, in a forest, on an island, in a swampy, steamy sea there lived a bunch of dinosaurs in happy harmony.

They picked the delicious vegetables and fruits growing wild in the forest, and stored them in a hollow tree stump to eat whenever they pleased. They read, and drew, and played games, too, like Dino-tag . . .

. . . and Rararagoo.

There was just one thing the dinosaurs lacked, and that was fire. With nothing to heat them or their food, it was tough keeping warm when winter rolled around. They munched on frozen bananas and chilled lettuce leaves, and waited patiently for spring.

But deep in the forest something even worse than winter was brewing. Something bad and very, very big.

CHAPTER THREE

One bright spring day, Dolores and
her friends were playing Dino-tag
around the Hooter tree, the biggest
tree in all the forest.

Suddenly, they heard a . . .

Louder and louder it grew.
Until ...

... smashing through the forest
towards them came a monstrous
beast!

A hundred jagged teeth lined his snarling mouth!

Ferocious fireballs flew from his flaring nostrils!

"HA!" he boomed.

The dinosaurs shuffled about
nervously.

spoke up Dolores. She believed that
you should never judge a book by
its cover, or even a monster by its
manner, and so she invited the
stranger to join them.

"Phoo!" he spat.
"Tag is a game for weeds and
wimps!"

But when they began to play, the
monster did not follow the rules.
He pushed Dolores around . . .

. . . he tripped up Terry . . .

. . . and toasted Tyrone with his blazing breath.

"Hmm . . ." Dolores mused.

Perhaps sometimes you _should_ judge a book by its cover!

CHAPTER FOUR

By the end of the afternoon the dinosaurs were battered, bruised and beaten.

"BAH!" bellowed the beast. "This is BORING!"

"Then go away!" said Theo bravely.

"How about if *you* go away?" the monster snarled, turning his cold, yellow eyes on Theo.

Grabbing Theo by the tail, he whirled him around and around his head.

"I feel sick!" Theo squealed. "Let me go!"

"If you insist!" the beast cackled.

Like a shot from a cannon, he
flew off over the forest . . .

. . . and Dolores could hold her
tongue no longer.

"That's right, Shorty!" sneered the
monster.

Bullysaurus swaggered over to the tree stump where the dinosaurs kept their food.

"Well, if I can't eat this," he hissed, "I'll just have to eat something else . . ."

The monster stuffed his cavernous mouth with food. Then, belching and burping balls of flame, he lumbered back into the forest, without even an 'excuse me' or a 'thank you'.

CHAPTER FIVE

spoke a little voice from behind a
bush.

"You can come out," said Tyrone.

Theo stepped forward. He was
dripping wet.

"I landed in the lake!" he
shivered.

His friends rushed around him,
dried him off, and did their best to
make him feel better . . .

. . . but what Theo needed was the one thing they didn't have; a roaring fire to warm him up. His cold got so bad, by nightfall his sneezes tore the leaves from the branches of the Hooter tree.

Dolores crossed her fingers and her toes. "I hope that's the last we see of Bullysaurus!" she wished.

Please, please may he NEVER come back!

Unfortunately, crossing your fingers and toes doesn't *always* work.

Bullysaurus would not leave them alone. Every day he came crashing through the forest, and every day he spoiled their fun . . .

. . . and ate their food.

By the end of the week, they all felt totally miserable.

"This can't go on!" Dinah wailed.

"It's hopeless!" groaned Terry

24

"What we lack in strength, we must make up in cunning!" said Dolores.

The dinosaurs sat in a circle and tried to think of a way to rid themselves of Bullysaurus.

They thought . . .

. . . and thought . . .

. . . and thought.

"Ouch!" moaned Dinah at daybreak. "I can't think anymore!"

"Forget it!" said Dolores, bouncing to her feet.

They gathered around in a huddle while Dolores whispered her plan.

"Hmm . . ." said Theo. "It's a long shot . . ."

CHAPTER SIX

The next day, Dinah, Dolores and Tyrone had just begun a game of Rararagoo, when . . .

Thundering out of the forest came Bullysaurus!

"Forget skipping rope!" he roared.
"Skip THIS!"

Just then, Terry flew down onto a branch of the Hooter tree. He was looking very worried.

"I saw a whirlwind!" Terry hissed.

"And . . . and . . ." Terry paused for breath.

Dolores gulped.

"FLEE!" she shrieked.

"It's useless!" howled Terry. "The whirlwind's moving faster than lightning! It'll be here any second! It'll suck us all up . . ."

"It's our only hope!" cried Dolores.

They fell silent. And then . . .

A burst of wind ripped through the forest!

Bullysaurus snatched the
Rararagoo ropes from Dolores.

The monster shoved them aside.
"Listen, creeps!" he growled.

CHAPTER SEVEN

The dinosaurs had no choice. As fast as they could, they lashed Bullysaurus to the tree.

Suddenly . . .

By the time the dinosaurs had
finished tying up Bullysaurus...

... there were no ropes left for
them!

Their bottom lips began to
tremble . . .

. . . their eyes filled with tears and
their shoulders began to shake . . .

"Cry-babies!" scoffed Bullysaurus.

But then, to his surprise . . .

They began to cry . . .

. . . with laughter!
Bullysaurus was astonished.
"What? Have you gone mad?"

"Whirlwind?" asked Dolores, wiping her eyes.

"The one bird-brain told us about!" bellowed Bullysaurus.

Suddenly . . .

"There it is again!" shouted
Bullysaurus.

Dolores cupped a hand around
her mouth.

"Hey, Theo!" she called into the
forest.

Out stepped Theo.

"A whirlwind? Of course not!" he laughed.

He lifted a finger to his nose.

And then Bullysaurus realised. At last.

CHAPTER EIGHT

"It wasn't a whirlwind at all!" seethed Bullysaurus. "It was you all along!"

He struggled to free himself, but he was bound up tight.

"You can spit fire and shout all you like," said Dinah, "but you're not going anywhere until you've learned some manners!"

"Suit yourself!" said Tyrone, and the dinosaurs walked away.

"I don't know about you," said Dolores to her friends . . .

But, instead of food in the tree stump, all they found was a blazing fire.

"Come closer," said Tyrone, "and feel for yourselves!"

The nights had been chilly, but curled up around the fire, the dinosaurs were warm as toast. One by one, they drifted off to sleep, happy in the knowledge that Bullysaurus could harm them no more.

CHAPTER NINE

In the deep of the night, Dolores woke up.

It wasn't coming from Theo. Or Dinah. Or even Tyrone or Terry. "Goodness me!" thought Dolores.

She left the warmth of the glowing embers, and crept over to the monster.

"Go away!" Bullysaurus whined.

"OK, OK!" said Dolores. "If that's what you want!"

Suddenly, tears the size of marbles bounced down Bullysaurus's leathery cheeks.

"I never wanted to be a bully!" he spluttered.

"But there must be something else you can do!" said Dolores.

Whenever Bullysaurus felt depressed there was just one thing that could cheer him up.

Dolores tiptoed over to the hollow tree stump.

She looked all around, but all she could find was one charred potato.

She took it over to Bullysaurus.

He took a bite . . .

It was the best thing Dolores had ever tasted! It wasn't hard and cold like normal potatoes. Underneath the crisp skin, it was soft and warm. "You know what, Bullysaurus?" Dolores chuckled.

CHAPTER TEN

Bullysaurus was very excited.

"I *said* you were good at
something other than bullying!"
said Dolores.

"Just loosen these ropes, and I'll
tell you!" he said.

Dolores wasn't sure . . .

She began to untie him, but as soon as the ropes had loosened a little . . .

CHAPTER ELEVEN

Theo woke up, stretched and looked about him.

When he saw the broken ropes by the Hooter tree he leapt to his feet. "The monster's escaped!" he shouted. "Departed! And Dolores . . ."

Suddenly . . .

From out of the forest walked
Dolores . . . and Bullysaurus,
carrying a huge tray of food!

"Don't be afraid!" grinned
Bullysaurus.

They didn't have to be asked
twice.

They devoured everything that Bullysaurus had prepared; treats like veggie kebabs, fire-roasted bananas and, of course, baked potatoes!

Meanwhile, Bullysaurus wandered through the forest searching for exciting new ingredients and dreaming up elaborate recipes.

With his new-found talent, he invented a thousand ways to cook fruit and vegetables. But of all of them, barbequing was his speciality, and so everyone agreed to call him Grill'O'Saurus!

With Theo's help he wrote down his hundred favourite recipes in an enormous book, for everyone to share.

And so, with fire to keep the cold away, and plenty to eat from salad to soufflé . . .

. . . In a forest, on an island, in a swampy, steamy sea, there lived a bunch of dinosaurs in happy harmony.

CHAPTER TWELVE

"And so ends the story of Bullysaurus," read Professor Water-Biscuit and Carlisle Withering. "And with it ends *my* story! I hope you enjoy the recipes as much as me!"

At the bottom of the page was this signature:

Grill'o'saurus

"What an incredible find!" Carlisle Withering gasped.

But the professor, who had just written a book called *The Whole Truth About Dinosaurs*, was very upset.

"No, you fool!" spat the professor. "Cover it back up with earth, and never tell a soul about it, that's what!"

And that's exactly what they did. For the truth is, we can never know the *whole* truth about dinosaurs. We can be sure of just one thing . . .

. . . that, once upon a time, when
the Universe was younger,
dinosaurs roamed our planet
Earth.

They came in many shapes,
colours and sizes – just like us. And
just like us, they laughed and cried
and lived and died, while the World
spun silently through space.